MW01101928

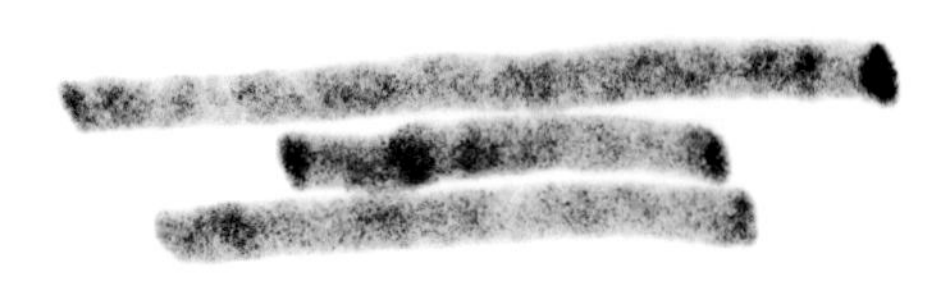

DRUGS the facts about

INHALANTS

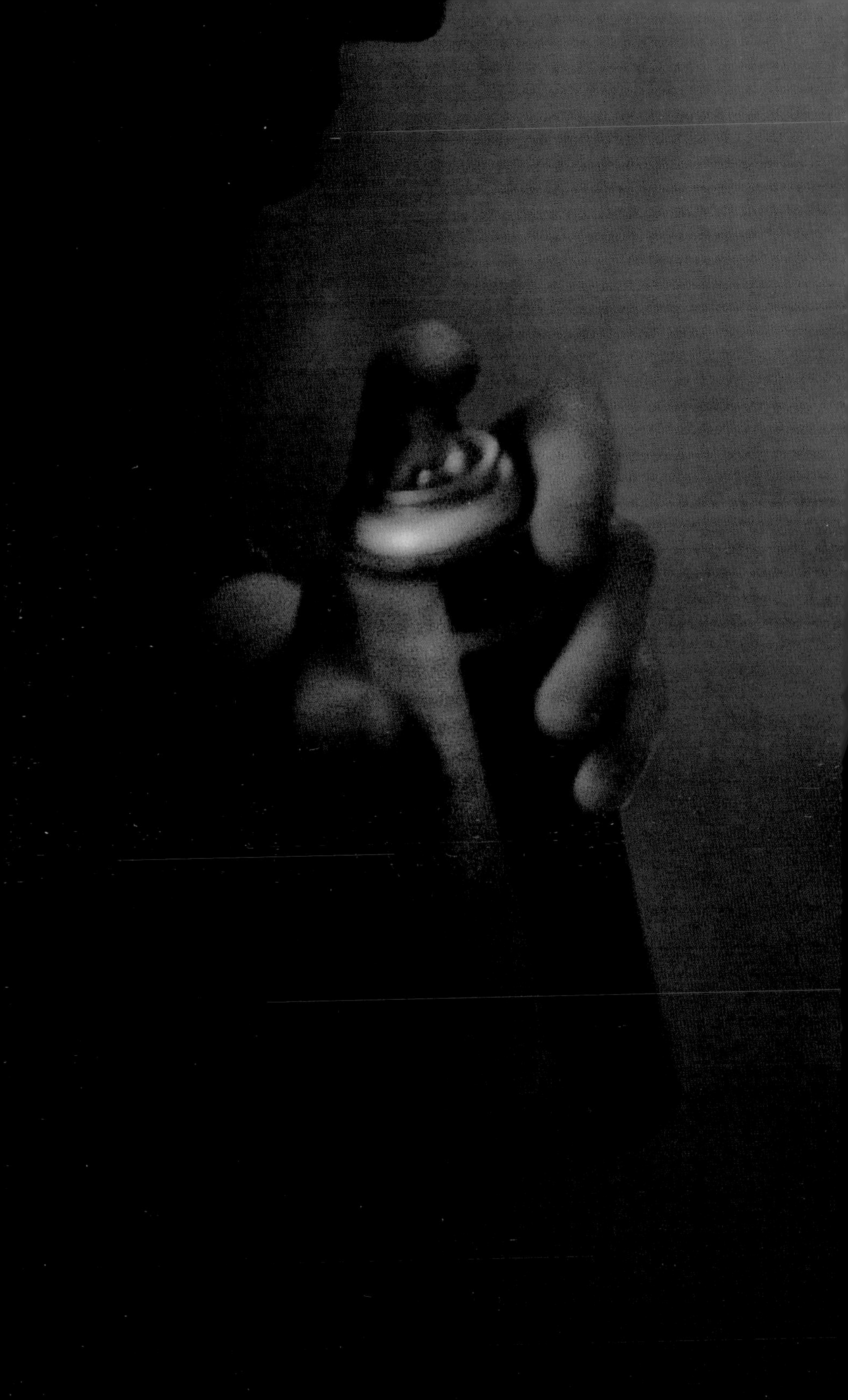

DRUGS

the facts about INHALANTS

FRANCHA ROFFÈ MENHARD

For the librarians at Athmar.

Series Consultant: Dr. Amy Kohn, Chief Executive Officer, YWCA of White Plains and Central Westchester, New York.
Thanks to John M. Roll, PhD, Director of Behavioral Pharmacology at UCLA Integrated Substance Abuse Programs, for his expert reading of this manuscript.

Benchmark Books
Marshall Cavendish
99 White Plains Road
Tarrytown, NY 10591-9001
www.marshallcavendish.us

All Internet sites were available and accurate when sent to press.

Library of Congress Cataloging-in-Publication Data

Menhard, Francha Roffe.
The facts about inhalants / Francha Roffe Menhard.
p. cm. – (Drugs)
Includes bibliographical references and index.
ISBN 0-7614-1809-1
1. Solvent abuse–Juvenile literature. 2. Aerosol sniffing–Juvenile literature.
I. Title. II. Series: Drugs (Benchmark Books (Firm))

RC568.S64M465 2005
362.29'9–dc22
2004011858

Photo research by Joan Meisel
Cover photo by Sonia Chaghatzbanian

Corbis: Bettmann, 63; 27, 29; AFP, 40; *Photo Researchers, Inc.*: Art Attack, 6 (bottom); Aaron Haupt, 6 (top); TEK Image, 11; Kul Bhatia, 42.

Printed in China
3 5 6 4

CONTENTS

1	What Are Inhalants?	7
2	A History of Inhalant Abuse	27
3	The Dangers of Inhalant Abuse	43
4	Help for Inhalant Abusers	63
5	Inhalants and the Law	72
	Glossary	78
	Further Information	80
	Index	85

Many teens do not realize inhalants are dangerous because they are found in so many household products. Inhalants may be cheap and legal when used as directed, but they can cause serious illness and even death.

1 What Are Inhalants?

THEY ARE UNDER the bathroom sink, in the kitchen cabinet, and in the garage. They are in the refrigerator and on the school secretary's desk. They are in the closet at school and at the dentist's office. They are inhalants, the drug of choice of elementary school students and one of the favorites of junior high and high school students. They go by such street names as glue, kick, bang, sniff, huff, poppers, whippets, and Texas shoeshine.

They are also the most commonly overlooked drugs in the United States today. Inhalants are cheap and easy to buy, so many people do not think of them as drugs. Can people really get high on hair spray, cooking spray, and gasoline? Do people really get addicted to cleaning fluid, or to aerosol-dispensed whipped cream? Can correction fluid harm the human body? Can the laughing gas dentists use to make patients less anxious really be dangerous?

The answer to all these questions is yes. Children, teens, and adults across the nation intentionally inhale the chemicals in these products to get high. Snorting inhalants from a container, bagging from a plastic or paper bag, and huffing volatile solvents from a rag—all of these can have serious effects on the body, especially the brain and the nervous system. Abusing inhalants does sometimes cause death, even the first time a person snorts, sniffs, or huffs.

According to the Office of National Drug Control Policy, the term *inhalants* "refers to more than a thousand household and commercial products that can be abused by inhaling them through one's mouth or nose for an intoxicating effect." These include volatile solvents—liquids that produce chemical gases at room temperature; adhesives, which are gluelike substances; lighter fluids; cleaning solvents; and nitrites—gas propellants found in aerosol room odorizers and paints. There are over a thousand products that can be inhaled. They are cheap and easy to come by and conceal, so inhalants are one of the first substances young people abuse.

Common Inhalants

Solvents

• Industrial or household solvents or products containing solvents, including paint thinners or removers, degreasers, dry-cleaning fluids, gasoline, and glue.

• Art- or office-supply solvents, including correction fluids, felt-tip-marker fluid, and some electronic-contact-cleaner solutions.

Gases

• Gases used in household or commercial products, including butane lighters and propane tanks, whipped cream aerosols or dispensers (whippets), and refrigerant gases.

• Household aerosol propellants and associated solvents in items such as spray paints, hair or deodorant sprays, and fabric-protector sprays.

• Medical anesthetic gases, such as ether, chloroform, halothane, and nitrous oxide (laughing gas).

Nitrites

• Aliphatic nitrites, including cyclohexyl nitrite, an ingredient found in room odorizers.

• Amyl nitrite, which is used for medical purposes.

• Butyl nitrite, previously used to manufacture perfumes and antifreeze, is now an illegal substance.

—Source: National Institute on Drug Abuse

Inhalants Are Different

Inhalants are different from other recreational drugs. Most recreational drugs—such as marijuana, cocaine, and heroin—are defined by their origin. But inhalants contain many different chemicals. The only thing inhalant chemicals have in common with each other is the way they enter the body. Users take in inhalants through their respiratory system—usually through the nose but sometimes through the mouth. Users of other recreational drugs generally know what drug they are introducing into their bodies. But it is almost impossible for inhalant users to know what chemicals they are breathing.

Different inhaled chemicals affect the body in different ways. Paint thinners, nail polish, and gasoline contain toluene (pronounced TALL u wen). Toluene mainly attacks the brain. Spray paint, air freshener, and lighter fluid contain butane and propane, which are the chemicals most likely to harm the heart and cause sudden death. Antifreeze, caulking compounds, and sealants contain trichloroethylene, which mainly attacks the heart and liver.

Less common recreational inhalants include medical anesthetic gases, such as ether, chloroform, halothane, and nitrous oxide; gases used for household or commercial products found in whipped cream dispensers, butane lighters, and refrigerants; aerosol propellants such as those in hair sprays and spray paints; and aliphatic nitrites used in some inks, rubbers, and adhesives.

The government regulates many of the chemicals in inhalants as environmental pollutants or industrial poisons. People who work around these chemicals know how dangerous they are, and they often wear special gear to protect themselves.

Inhalants are different from other drugs in other ways as well. People often fail to recognize that inhalants are drugs, since most inhaled products were never meant to be used for getting high. Most inhalants are legal when people use them properly.

They are safe when people follow the warnings on their labels. These warnings are important because the chemicals in these products are poisonous in high doses. And inhalants are available everywhere. They are cheap to buy and easy to pick up for free at school and at home. This is not true of most recreational drugs. Cocaine, heroin, methamphetamines, and Ecstasy do not have legal uses. The laws against them are straightforward.

Inhalants have not been as thoroughly researched as other drugs of abuse. Doctors know what to do when someone comes into the emergency room overdosing on heroin or cocaine. Treatment centers for other drugs have been around for a long time, and have well-developed treatment practices. Some of the chemicals in inhalants have been well researched—especially those that government agencies have regulated as environmental pollutants or industrial toxins (poisons). But since there are so many chemicals that can be inhaled, thorough research will take a long, long time. And unless medical personnel know exactly what chemicals an inhalant abuser took before arriving at an emergency room, they can never be sure of exactly what to do.

Finally, alcohol and drug treatment centers do not work well for people hooked on inhalants, because inhalant abuse is such a complicated addiction. In 2003 there was only one center in the United States specifically for the treatment of inhalant abusers, in Bethel, Alaska.

Street Slang for Inhalants

Inhalants
Air blast
Discorama
Hippie crack
Honey oil
Huff
Kick
Medusa
Moon gas
Oz
Poor man's pot
Quicksilver
Rush
Sniff
Toilet water
Whiteout

Using Inhalants
Bagging
Glading
Huffing
Snorting

Inhalant user
Gluey (one who inhales glue)

Amyl nitrite
Ames
Amys
Boppers
Pearls
Poppers

Isobutyl nitrite
Aroma of men
Bolt
Climax
Hardware
Poppers
Quicksilver
Rush
Snappers
Thrust
Whiteout

Nitrous oxide
Buzz bomb
Laughing gas
Shoot the breeze
Whippets

–Source: Drug Policy Information Clearinghouse

Signs of Abuse

Adults often overlook the signs of inhalant use. If they never tried inhalants when they were young, the idea barely registers on their radar screen. Could their child really be breathing spray paint to get high? Can people really abuse the nitrous oxide—laughing gas—that dentists use to help patients relax? It does not seem possible. Not only that, the signs of inhalant abuse are easy for adults to miss and easy for young people to explain away.

For example, Shari's parents did not notice when she started buying twelve-packs of correction fluid. And when Bob's mom got suspicious of the chemical fumes coming from his room, he told her that he was working on a science project. Other parents have noticed paint stains on clothes and rags—or socks, bags, or rags that smell of chemicals—and failed to realize that they could be signs of inhalant abuse.

Who Uses Inhalants?

Inhalants are an equal opportunity drug. People who live in cities and rural areas abuse inhalants at about the same rate as do different racial groups. However, there are some small differences. For example, American Indian youths who live on reservations, where socioeconomic distress and school dropout rates are high, typically have higher rates of inhalant abuse than both the general population of young people and those American Indian youths who do not live on reservations. Economic status is a more important determining factor than racial or cultural factors. Young people who have suffered poverty or a history of physical or sexual abuse during childhood, and those with consistently poor grades, including dropouts, are more likely to abuse inhalants in the long term. Many more boys than girls experiment with inhalants in grades four through six. In grades seven through nine, boys and girls use inhalants equally. In high school, boys again are more likely to use inhalants. In the eighteen- to twenty-five-year range, males are twice as likely to continue abusing inhalants than do females.

These data raise questions. How is it that in almost every survey fewer twelfth graders than eighth graders consistently report they have ever abused inhalants? Have high school seniors forgotten the use of inhalants that they reported on earlier surveys? Were they lying on earlier surveys to try to look cool? Or do many eighth-grade inhalant abusers drop out of school before twelfth grade and thus are no longer around to answer survey questions about inhalant use? Research shows that dropouts and students with poor grades have higher rates of inhalant abuse than their classmates who make better grades and stay in school.

Parents Are Clueless

Ricky's parents talked with him openly about anything and everything. They warned him about the dangerous consequences of using drugs and alcohol. But they never, not one single time, warned Ricky about the dangers of huffing.

Why? Because they had never heard of huffing.

Ricky's parents have spent more than five years explaining to other parents how their son died. When they say, "He died huffing," parents ask, "Huffing, what is huffing?"

Seth Bramley's mother remembers finding washcloths with the outline of her son's face. They smelled like air freshener. She never had any idea what the washcloths meant. Seth told his mother, "Mom, I so much want to live. I don't want to get high, but I just can't stop." Then he held her hand and promised not to abuse inhalants ever again. It was a promise he could not keep. Just days later, he bagged a can of shaving gel and died with the plastic bag over his head.

"Seth was no longer in control," said Mrs. Bramley McCormick. "The inhalants had taken over his life." Nine out of ten parents are unaware that their children have ever abused inhalants, according to the Partnership for a Drug-Free America. The U.S. Consumer Product Safety Commission puts that number even higher. Their survey showed that 95 percent of parents believe their child has never abused inhalants.

What kind of individuals abuse inhalants? According to National Inhalant Prevention Coalition treatment guidelines, there are four personality categories. *Transient social users* are generally people of average intelligence between the ages of ten and sixteen. They use inhalants for a short time, in the company of friends. *Chronic social users* are those people between twenty and thirty years old who have used inhalants daily with their friends for five years or more. Outside of this group, they have poor social skills. They usually have limited education and show signs of brain damage from their inhalant use and have probably had minor run-ins with the law. *Transient isolate users* are generally between the ages of ten and sixteen and have used inhalants by themselves for a short period of time. *Chronic isolates* are between twenty and thirty years old and have used inhalants daily for five or more years. They use inhalants by themselves and generally have poor social skills and limited education. They show signs of brain damage from their inhalant use and have probably had minor run-ins with the law.

Why Do People Use Inhalants?

For some young people the appeal of getting high is too strong to resist. Others are curious, and just want to try inhalants. Still others cannot say no to peers who pressure them to inhale deadly chemicals. Inhalants are easily available to teens. They are

Some Symptoms of Acute Inhalant Intoxication

Neurological (affecting the nervous system)

- euphoria (an exaggerated feeling of physical and mental well-being)
- auditory and visual hallucinations
- slurring of speech
- loss of muscular coordination
- double vision
- tremors

Pulmonary (affecting the lungs)

- shortness of breath, difficulty breathing
- wheezing
- coughing
- bluish discoloration of the arms and legs

cheap and easy to hide. They are also legal, so teens are less likely to be arrested than if they were using marijuana, crack cocaine, or other illegal drugs.

In some cases, young people turn to inhalants in order to numb the pain of a difficult life. Some have poor social skills, few friends, and a strong feeling of hopelessness and isolation. Others have been physically or sexually abused. Yet others are reeling in the aftermath of a divorce or a death in the family.

Many teens do not realize how dangerous inhalants are at first, or they deny the danger to themselves. Once hooked, they may realize that inhalants cannot solve their problems. And they find out that inhalants can be addictive, both psychologically and physically. Inhalant abuse is a tough habit to break.

Addictive Recreation

Inhalants can be addicting. Regardless of how they get started, people who are long-term abusers of inhalants continue because they like the immediate high, a feeling similar to the intoxication alcohol creates. They keep on inhaling because it feels good. Furthermore, some people who abuse inhalants do build up a tolerance. They have to inhale more and more to get the same high as before. Some develop cravings for their inhalant of choice, and many experience irritability, trouble sleeping, nausea, and tremors when they try to kick the habit. These symptoms are common in withdrawal from many drugs.

Just how addictive inhalants can be was a surprise to researchers. In the past, most people believed that the chemicals in inhalants spread uniformly throughout the body. However, improved technology has made it possible to put that theory to the test. In recent experiments researchers attached a radioactive marker to toluene molecules, one of the most common chemicals in inhalants, and injected mice and baboons. The researchers then followed the migration of the radioactive toluene molecules by taking positron-emission tomography (PET) scans. Researchers also collected tissue samples to confirm what they saw in the PET scans.

To their surprise, they discovered that the toluene molecules headed straight for the brain. There, they activated the brain's dopamine system, just as cocaine and heroin do. Dopamine is a neurotransmitter—a chemical that transmits nerve impulses—that contributes to creating feelings of pleasure and euphoria, the high that drug users seek. The molecules then spread throughout the entire brain and quickly left the body through the kidneys.

At the same time they are producing pleasure, inhalant chemicals are dissolving the nerves in the brain, according to Dr. Janet F. Williams, a member of the American Academy of Pediatrics Committee on Substance Abuse. This damage to the nervous system is not reversible. Even when inhalant abusers understand the damage that can be done to the brain, the pleasure that inhalants produce may make it difficult to quit.

Tragedy Strikes Media, PA

The deaths of five teens outside Media, Pennsylvania, was just one example of how inhalants kill and of the heartbreak they cause. Students at Penncrest High School left school at noon the last Friday in January 1999. Five girlfriends went to the mall to shop for dresses for their junior prom, just two weeks away. Just before 4 p.m., their car swerved out of control on a stretch of road that locals call Dead Man's Curve and slammed into a pole and a tree.

By the time rescuers got the girls out of the car, four of them were dead. The fifth passenger, Tracy Graham, was airlifted to the University of Pennsylvania Hospital, where she died. The car was traveling between 66 and 88 miles per hour when it hit the pole, and an officer found a can of Duster II, a spray used to clean computer keyboards, inside the car. An autopsy showed traces of the chemical difluoroethane in the blood of four of the girls, including the driver. "Intoxication in the driver developed to the point that she could no longer control the car," Medical Examiner Dimitri Contostavlos reported. The parents of the girls were stunned. The girls must have inhaled the spray unintentionally, they agreed.

Death by Inhalants

No one knows exactly how many teens die from inhalants each year, because no one keeps accurate statistics. Furthermore, inhalant deaths are often attributed to other causes. Inhalants were a factor in more than five hundred deaths in forty metropolitan areas in the United States between 1996 and 1999, according to Drug Abuse Warning Network (DAWN) data collected from coroners and medical examiners, among others. That works out to around one hundred twenty-five deaths per year. That statistic puts inhalants way down on the list of causes of death for teens.

Although the number of inhalant deaths is low, damage is devastating and irreversible. "It's a crapshoot," says Dr. H. Westley Clark of the Substance Abuse and Mental Health Services Administration. "You're risking your life, you're risking your heart, you're risking your kidneys, you're risking your brain."

Death by inhalants can occur in a number of ways—including asphyxiation, in which the inhalant gas replaces oxygen to the lungs, causing breathing to stop. Users may also choke on their own vomit or cover their nose and mouth with plastic bags and lose awareness before they can remove them, leading to suffocation. Some inhalant users lose their good sense while high and become involved in accidents or homicide. Some commit suicide or die while engaged in dangerous behavior. And finally, several teens each year are victims of Sudden Sniffing Death syndrome (SSD), in which the heart beats irregularly and then stops.

The oracle at Delphi handed down prophecies to the Greeks after inhaling sweet vapors that drifted into her chamber at the temple of Apollo. The oracle may have been an early inhalant user, breathing in gases that drifted up from a crack in the rocks below the temple.

2 A History of Inhalant Abuse

PEOPLE HAVE BEEN using inhalants as an intoxicant since the time of the ancient Greeks. For about a thousand years the oracle at Delphi handed down prophecies to ancient Greeks and Roman rulers. The oracle was chosen from among the local women. From her chamber at the Temple of Apollo in Delphi, she gave advice and foretold the future for the citizens of ancient Greece and Rome.

The Greek writer Plutarch wrote about how the oracle would inhale the sweet-smelling vapors that drifted into her chamber. Then she would go into a trance. Sometimes the fumes caused a frenzy, and some oracles even died. Plutarch believed that the sacred fumes the oracle was inhaling were actually gases that escaped from a fissure, or crack, in the rocks below the temple. He suspected that nearby earthquakes probably released the fumes. Modern geologists tell us that Plutarch was right. Theodosius I, the emperor of Rome, banned the oracle in 392 C.E., but people continued to inhale mind-altering gases.

Around 1800 Humphry Davy, an English chemist, realized that a newly discovered gas, nitrous oxide, had mind-altering effects. Not realizing that the gas could have dangerous side effects, Davy held private nitrous oxide parties for his friends. Soon, inhaling nitrous oxide was all the rage. Traveling shows let people pay to experience the effects of the gas. They called it laughing gas because it made them giddy and giggly. "I am sure the air in heaven must be this wonder-working gas of delight," English poet Robert Southey wrote about his experience with nitrous oxide.

In the 1840s doctors discovered that ether and chloroform could render patients unconscious for surgery. They also found that these drugs produced a high and demonstrated them to the public at parties called ether frolics. All the feelings were not good, however. In 1848 Dr. Horace Wells threw acid on the clothing of a prostitute while under the influence of chloroform. Days later, he slashed his thigh with a razor in his cell at Tombs prison and died at age thirty-three.

The famous poet and painter Dante Gabriel Rossetti, who became addicted to ether, also died

The English chemist, Humphry Davy, discovered that nitrous oxide had mind-altering effects. People called it laughing gas because it made them giddy and giggly. Guests at Davy's parties inhaled the gas, not realizing that it could harm them.

young, his health destroyed by his addiction. The Industrial Revolution of the eighteenth century introduced the use of a whole new host of chemicals to the production of goods, and volatile solvents began to appear in more and more products used in factories, homes, and offices. Newly invented motors used oil and diesel fuel. The invention of the automobile introduced gasoline.

After World War II, a number of products became widespread in the U.S. making life simpler. People could easily buy paint thinner, spray paint, deodorant, hair spray, cleaning fluid, refrigerant gases, cooking gases, tobacco-lighter gases, canned whipped cream, dust-remover aerosols, and fabric protectors. In 1956 Liquid Paper, the first correction fluid, hit the market. Each new invention meant new inhalants to abuse. Most people did not deliberately breathe the fumes, and those who did failed to realize how dangerous they were. In fact, it was only when workers began getting sick after exposure to inhalants in the workplace that people realized that these chemicals could be dangerous.

Glue Sniffing Becomes Popular

Before 1959 inhaling volatile substances was not a social problem. It was something that only a handful of people did. Then widespread media attention helped create a glue-sniffing epidemic.

On August 2, 1959, the *Denver Post* ran a story about the arrest of several children in Pueblo,

Colorado, and Tucson, Arizona, for sniffing glue. The story went on to explain in detail how one inhales glue and the effects:

> The first effect of breathing the undiluted fumes is dizziness, followed by drowsiness. There is a feeling of suspension of reality. Later there is lack of coordination of muscle and mind.

The story made sniffing glue sound just like getting drunk. Young people wanted to try out this new high. By June 1960 Denver police had investigated some fifty cases of glue sniffing. Later stories warned young people against sniffing glue.

Unfortunately, this additional media coverage did not end the glue-sniffing menace. In fact, the opposite happened. The epidemic spread. By October 23, 1961, the Denver Juvenile Court was dealing with about thirty young glue sniffers a month, up from zero just a few years before.

In 1962 the Hobby Industry Association produced a fifteen-minute film, *The Scent of Danger.* The film described the ill effects glue sniffing could have on the body and recommended stiff, new laws. The warnings did not slow the growth of glue sniffing. Glue sales increased. The warnings got stronger. Police spokesmen and legislators warned that glue fumes diminished the oxygen supply to the blood and could permanently damage the brain and even cause death.

But scientific research did not support these findings. Dr. Oliver Massengale, director of the Adolescent Clinic at the University of Colorado Medical Center, and Dr. Helen Glaser, assistant professor of pediatrics, conducted scientific research on recreational glue sniffing. Their research, published in the *Journal of the American Medical Association* in 1962, indicated that some types of plastic cement could cause damage to the liver, kidneys, and brain only as a result of swallowing large amounts of glue or continuous, day-after-day exposure to high concentrations by workers in industrial plants. This did not bear out the dire warnings of the newspaper articles.

"Although a great deal of concern about the ill effects of this practice is expressed by parents, school personnel, juvenile authorities, and the children themselves," Glaser and Massengale wrote, "very little is actually known about possible damage to organ systems resulting from deliberate inhalation of cement vapors." They also stated that they had found only one case in which a teen used glue in an attempt to commit suicide.

For the rest of the decade, glue sniffing continued to spread to other parts of the country, as did arrests, new laws, and new research studies. Surveys showed just how popular glue sniffing had become. Surveys of high schools and junior high schools in the late 1960s found that at least 5 percent of students had tried sniffing glue, in contrast to ten years earlier, when most teens and adults had never heard about glue sniffing.

On July 20, 1971, the *New York Times* began another nationwide anti-inhalant campaign, this time against aerosol sniffing. "Physicians, government officials, drug experts and chemical manufacturers are growing increasingly worried about a deadly and relatively new drug-abuse problem among the nation's children: the inhalation of aerosol sprays," Grace Lichtenstein reported in the *New York Times*.

The article, like those before it in *Newsweek* and *Time* magazines, warned of the dangers of sniffing glue and ran complete with a description of how to get high on aerosols. It also included which products were most popular and a warning about sudden death:

> According to the Food and Drug Administration, more than one hundred youths have died from deliberate aerosol sniffing since 1967, with an average of four deaths a month currently being recorded. . . . It appears that death occurs after a youngster deeply inhales an aerosol spray for a prolonged period, either on a single occasion or on several occasions. The fluorocarbon propellant Freon, the best-known brand of fluorocarbon, can make the heart beat irregularly and then stop. Once the final event begins, the article quoted an expert, it's quick, sudden, and irreversible.

The Scope of Inhalant Abuse

Beginning in 1965, the Substance Abuse and Mental Health Services Administration (SAMHSA) began keeping data on the abuse of inhalants to find out how many thousands of people had tried inhalants and at what age they had their first experience with inhalants. Their data shows how the number of inhalant abusers has increased in the thirty-five years since SAMHSA began keeping records, and also the increasing number of teens under the age of eighteen who are inhaling. Here are the results of this research.

Numbers (in Thousands) of Persons Who First Used Inhalants Including Mean Age at First Use

Year	All Ages	Under 18	18 or Older	Mean Age
1965	86	75	*	13.2
1966	190	190	*	13.8
1967	142	65	*	18.4
1968	237	143	*	17.7
1969	251	173	78	17.0
1970	291	198	94	16.8
1971	317	263	54	14.8
1972	284	158	126	18.8
1973	432	263	169	19.1
1974	532	290	243	18.0
1975	567	408	159	15.9
1976	584	336	248	17.0
1977	927	370	557	19.3
1978	690	373	317	18.1
1979	927	503	424	17.9
1980	659	369	290	19.3
1981	594	302	292	18.6
1982	636	369	267	17.7
1983	683	417	266	17.7
1984	583	343	240	18.3
1985	565	251	314	20.3
1986	556	352	204	19.5
1987	578	365	213	17.6
1988	651	370	281	17.6
1989	596	287	310	19.1
1990	488	266	222	17.8
1991	494	284	210	17.7
1992	631	405	226	17.0
1993	677	411	266	17.3
1994	627	429	198	16.6
1995	682	447	235	16.4
1996	708	446	262	17.0
1997	769	482	287	16.7
1998	935	548	386	17.5
1999	1,013	642	371	16.5
2000	1,247	865	382	16.5
2001	1,125	802	323	15.7

*Low precision; no estimate reported.

—Source: SAMHSA, Office of Applied Studies, National Survey on Drug Use and Health, 1999–2001.

One of the more popular aerosols, a spray-on product used to chill cocktail glasses, was quickly taken off store shelves in 1967 even though, as Lichtenstein reported, "any of the 300 kinds of aerosol products now on the market can be equally abused because all use similar propellants." Quickly, the aerosol industry produced a filmstrip and a booklet on the dangers of aerosol abuse to be distributed to schools, and legislators proposed new laws requiring a warning label on all aerosol products.

Inhalant Abuse Today

The abuse of inhalants is a problem in the United States and throughout the world. Inhalants are often the first substance children use to get high. Young teens are most likely to begin using inhalants because they are curious. Some say that their peer group pressured them into starting. Others say they started because they were bored or wanted to rebel against the adults in their lives. Some young users say they had never heard of inhalants and had no idea that sniffing the fumes of common household products could be dangerous.

How many people are abusing inhalants? No one can be sure, since most inhalant abuse is never reported. However, surveys show that nearly one in five young people will experiment with inhalants before they graduate from high school, according to Dr. H. Westley Clark of the Substance Abuse and Mental Health Services Administration.

Almost 10 percent of the U.S. population age twelve and older—18,219,000 people—said that they had used an inhalant at least once in their lifetime, according to the 2002 Monitoring the Future study. Three-quarters of all inhalant users are between ages twelve and twenty-five. Of twelfth graders 11.7 percent had used an inhalant in their lifetime, and 1.5 percent of twelfth graders, 2.4 percent of tenth, and 3.8 percent of eighth graders had used inhalants in the past month.

Until 1995, when almost 22 percent of eighth graders surveyed had tried inhalants in their lifetime, the problem was on the rise. By 2002, according to the study, the number had decreased to only 15.2 percent of eighth graders, 13.5 percent of tenth graders, and 11.7 percent of twelfth graders reporting that they had used inhalants in their lifetime.

The decrease in inhalant use is encouraging. So are the indications that campaigns to educate young people about the dangers of inhalants are working. Since 1985 the number of students who realize that inhalants can be dangerous is up. In 2000, 69.9 percent of eighth graders and 75 percent of tenth graders viewed regular inhalant use as dangerous. In addition, 41.2 percent of eighth graders and 46.6 percent of tenth graders thought using inhalants once or twice was dangerous. Most students not only realized that inhalants can be dangerous but also overwhelmingly disapproved of inhalant abuse—90.2 percent of eighth graders and 91.8 percent of tenth graders disapproved or strongly disapproved of using inhalants regularly, while 85.4 percent of eighth graders and 87.5 percent of tenth graders disapproved or strongly disapproved of using inhalants once or twice.

Victims of Inhalant Abuse in Central America

Across Central America tens of thousands of street children—some as young as five and six years old—sniff glue and other industrial solvents. Many of the children are orphans. Some have parents who are too poor to take care of themselves, let alone their children. They eat from dumpsters, sleep in cardboard boxes, keep their distance from police, and beg for small change to buy toluene-based glue from black marketers, who sell it from 55-gallon drums.

"Glue sniffing is a very pragmatic response of the children to the situation they're in. They need food, they need clothing, they need to be respected as human beings," says Bruce Harris, director of Casa Alianza, a shelter for street children. "We see five-year-olds with their heads stuck in plastic bags because it takes away their hunger, it keeps them warm, and it replaces their teddy bear."

Some of the children talked to *Honduras This Week* online reporter W. E. Gutman: Thirteen-year-old Luisa has been sniffing glue for three years. Sniffing glue helps her forget she is cold, hungry, and homeless. "When I feel nothing, I feel good," Luisa said.

Fourteen-year-old Amanda sniffed glue during both her pregnancies. Her first daughter was born dead. There was no way Amanda could take care of her second daughter, who suffers from seizures, so she abandoned her.

Ten-year-old Sergio has been sleeping on the streets for almost half his life. He sniffs glue to dull his hunger. Not long before Sergio spoke to Gutman, an angry policeman poured glue on his head. Some of the glue ran into one of his eyes and burned the cornea.

Joel Jesus Linares Polanco died on January 4, 1993, before he reached the age of seventeen. For years he lived on the mean streets of Guatemala. He started sniffing glue when he was eight years old. He and his brother used to sing on buses for change to buy food and glue. By the end of his life, he only did glue. It kept the hunger away.

By the end of his life, Joel couldn't taste food anyway. The inhalants had destroyed his sense of taste, along with most of his vital organs. He died from kidney failure in a halfway house in Guatemala City.

–Source: Minneapolis Star Tribune *and* HondurasThisWeek *online*

Young children forced to live on the streets in Central America do not have food, shelter, or teddy bears. Instead, they turn drugs to mask their hunger, keep them warm, and help them forget the grimness of their lives.

The Partnership for a Drug-Free America, which began a campaign in 1995 to educate young people about the dangers of inhalants, showed similar results in their 2002 Partnership Attitude Tracking Survey. In 2002, 19 percent of teens said that they had experimented with inhalants, down from 23 percent in 1995, when the education campaign began. Ten percent reported using inhalants in the past year, down from 16 percent in 1995, and 6 percent reported using inhalants in the past month, down from 8 percent in 1995.

Although the number of users continues to decrease, almost a million young people reported experimenting with inhalants, risking sudden death, in 2001.

Inhalants can cause death even the first time someone tries them. Inhalant users most often die from suffocation, preventable accidents, or Sudden Sniffing Death Syndrome, which causes the heart to stop beating.

3 The Dangers of Inhalant Abuse

INHALANT ABUSE IS especially dangerous because many young people assume the substances are safe, since they are available everywhere and are not banned, as other drugs are. Technically, inhalants are not drugs at all. "They are poisons" says Dr. Harvey Weiss, director of the National Inhalant Prevention Coalition in Austin, Texas.

Effects of Inhalant Abuse

Inhalants produce much the same psychoactive (mind-altering) effects as alcohol and other drugs do. Most inhalants create a short-lived high, then

depress or lower the ability of the body's vital systems to function. They attack the nervous system and the brain. Because they are inhaled rather than swallowed, they take effect more quickly than alcohol or barbiturates—within about five minutes.

Following the initial high, inhalants typically produce drowsiness, dizziness, slurred speech, slowed reflexes, apathy, inability to make good judgments, loss of inhibition (conscious or unconscious restraint of behavior), loss of sensation, muscle weakness, seizures, stupor, and unconsciousness. Some people become belligerent as the high wears off.

Long-term exposure to inhalants can cause serious and irreversible damage to the brain, including the areas that control movement, vision, hearing, and thinking. Some inhalant abusers have a hard time with coordination. Their arms and legs may become spastic. They may lose their hearing or vision. Others lose their ability to organize their thoughts or recall words. A few sink into dementia. Chronic inhalant abuse can also damage other important organs, including the heart, lungs, liver, kidneys, and bone marrow. This damage may not be reversible. Inhaling toxic chemicals while pregnant can damage the developing fetus and cause lifelong problems for the child. Prolonged sniffing of high concentrations of chemicals can cause rapid, irregular heartbeat, which can lead to heart failure and death.

But these are only generalities. Each chemical in

an inhalant has its own molecular structure, which causes unique symptoms and aftereffects. This makes it hard for users to know exactly what they are introducing into their bodies. They play a dangerous game of chance with their health. They may be fine, or they may lose their ability to walk normally or lose their hearing for the rest of their lives. They may die, even the first time they experiment with inhalants.

Most of the favorite recreational inhalants are classified and regulated by governments around the world as industrial toxins. They can cause illness and injury to workers even in relatively small concentrations. In fact, most of the early research on inhalants grew out of incidents of industrial poisoning.

Before the 1900s most employers were not too concerned about workplace safety and employee health. But when workers realized their jobs were making them sick, they joined together to demand better working conditions. That is when governments began to pass laws to protect workers from poisonous chemicals at their jobs. Today, occupational health and safety agencies such as the Occupational Safety and Health Administration (OSHA), National Institute for Occupational Safety and Health (NIOSH), and the Canadian Centre for Occupational Health and Safety publish warnings and regulate the amount of toxic chemicals in the air in the workplace.

Damage to the Body Caused by Inhalants

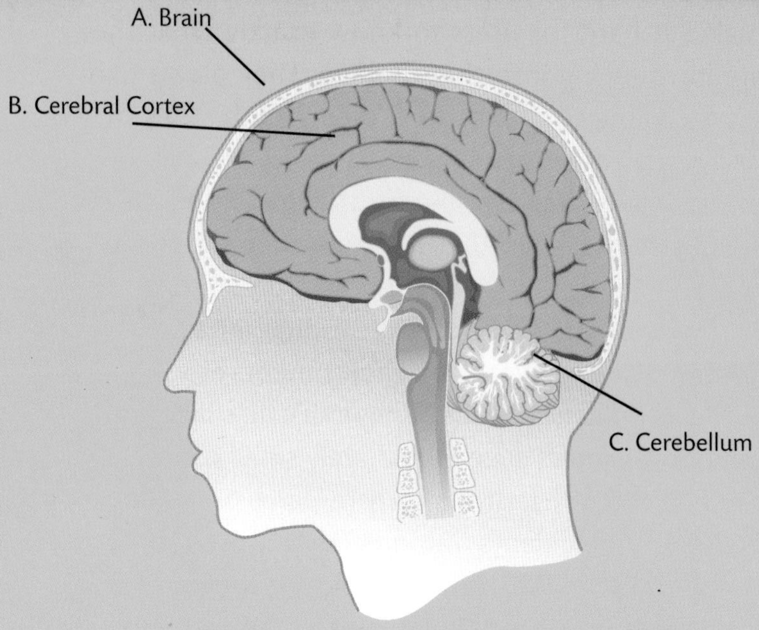

A. Brain The chemicals abused by inhalant users affect different parts of the brain. Many inhalants are thought to dissolve the protective myelin sheath that surrounds brain cells.

B. Cerebral Cortex Cellular death here causes permanent personality changes, memory impairment, hallucinations, and learning disabilities.

C. Cerebellum Damage to the center that controls balance and coordination results in loss of coordination and slurred speech. Chronic abusers experience tremors and shaking.

D. Blood The oxygen-carrying capacity of the blood may be inhibited.

E. Lungs Damaged lungs and impaired breathing occur with repeated use.

F. Heart SSD* syndrome, an unexpected disturbance in the heart's rhythm, may cause fatal cardiac arrhythmias (heart failure).

G. Liver Gathering of toxins in fatty tissue may cause liver damage.

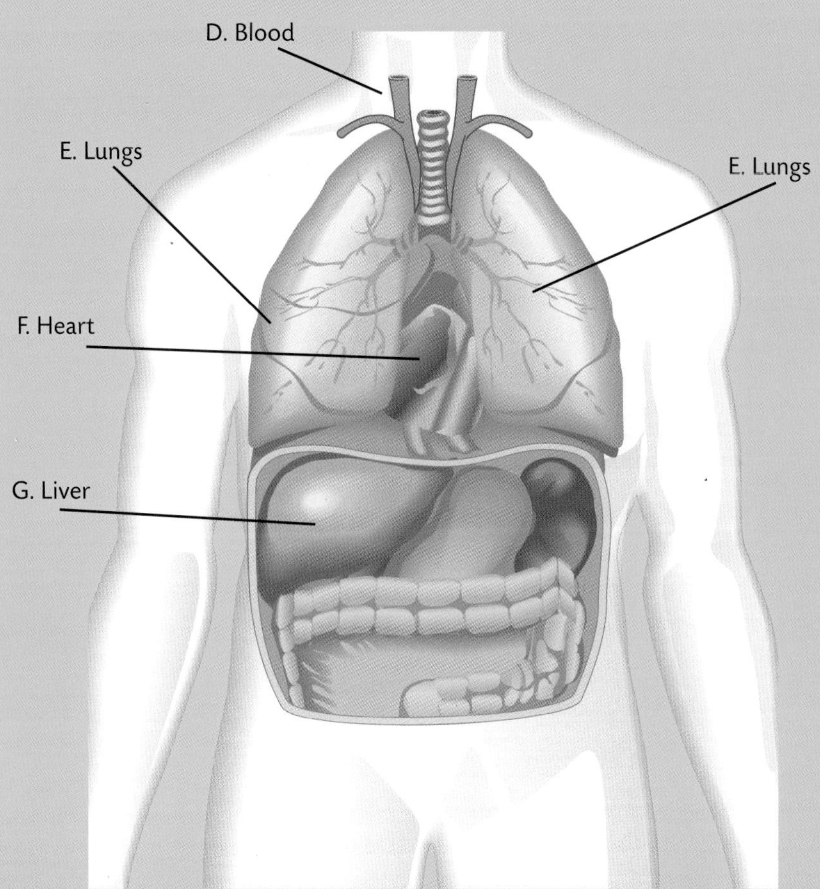

Other damage includes:

Acoustic nerve and muscle Destruction of cells that relay sound to the brain. May cause deafness.

Bone marrow Components containing benzene have been shown to cause leukemia

Muscle Chronic use may lead to muscle wasting and reduced muscle tone and strength.

Skin A sever rash around the nose and mouth, referred to as glue sniffer's rash, may result.

*SSD syndrome may result when a user deeply inhales a chemical for the effect of intoxication. This causes a decrease in available oxygen in the body. If the user becomes startled or engages in sudden physical activity, an increased flow of adrenaline to the heart induces cardiac arrest, and death occurs within minutes.

–Source: National Inhalant Prevention Coalition.

These warnings are convincing evidence that in much higher doses these same chemicals can be very dangerous to recreational inhalant users. The higher the dose, the more severe are the health effects. All inhalants cause similar reactions. But further studies point out how they differ from each other. There are three categories of inhalants—volatile solvents, gases, and nitrites.

Solvents

These are found in paint thinners, degreasers, gasoline, glues, correction fluid, and paint.

Toluene

Toluene is a clear, colorless liquid with a strong, sweet, and pungent odor. It occurs in processed oil. The body's fatty organs—the lungs, brain, heart, liver, and reproductive organs—absorb toluene quickly. In fact, shortly after inhalation, concentrations of toluene may be ten times greater in the brain than in the blood. Breathing high levels of toluene over long periods at work, or deliberately inhaling products that contain toluene, can cause depression; damage to the kidney, liver, nervous system, heart, and brain; unconsciousness; and even death. Toluene can be harmful to unborn babies.

Toluene is one of the most common and toxic chemicals in inhalants, and inhalant abusers often breathe in toluene at levels hundreds of times higher than the limits set for safety in the workplace. Toluene causes giddiness, loss of coordination, then headache.

A thirteen-year-old in east Tennessee became addicted to huffing paint. He knew he couldn't kick this addiction on his own. For seven years his parents put him in one treatment center after another to help him break his addiction. None of the programs worked, and the boy committed suicide.

Toluene is a severe fire hazard. Because its fumes are heavier than air, they may ignite unexpectedly and cause flash fires.

Studies prove that toluene damages the protective sheath around nerve fibers in the brain. This protective sheath is called myelin, and it operates something like insulation that wraps electrical wiring. Without the myelin sheath intact, toluene abusers may suffer some of the symptoms that multiple sclerosis victims suffer, such as depression, loss of cognitive ability, numbness and loss of feeling, vision disturbances, loss of coordination, and difficulty walking.

Gasoline

Gasoline is a mixture of a number of chemicals. As such, it is probably the least pure of the substances that people inhale. Gasoline is a colorless liquid with strong odor. Its yellowish color at the gas pump comes from dye. Gasoline is extremely flammable both as a liquid and as a vapor.

Gasoline is toxic as well as explosive and combustible. Inhaling gasoline fumes can depress the central nervous system, causing a short high. It can also cause headache, nausea, dizziness, drowsiness, unconsciousness, and death. Even if a person does not react strongly to the fumes, gasoline can impair judgment. Some people have failed to realize that smoking tobacco or other drugs while inhaling gasoline can cause serious burns or that accidentally swallowing or vomiting gasoline while inhaling could cause a person to breathe the liquid into the lungs. Based on animal tests, gasoline can cause cancer.

Gasoline is full of toxic chemicals, and each chemical is much more deadly when inhaled delib-

Three girls—Fallon Brown, age sixteen; her sister Brandie, thirteen; and their friend Shelly Franklin, twelve—died in a flash fire in Oklahoma. They had known about the dangers of inhalants. Their schools had begun warning students of inhalants in fifth grade. Fallon and Brandie's mother had found Fallon inhaling gasoline and had warned her against it. Still, the girls had locked themselves in a small, tightly sealed room, along with their bicycles, a radio, a space heater, and the can of gasoline. Fire investigators believe the space heater ignited the gasoline fumes, causing the fire. All three girls died of smoke inhalation.

erately than in industrial settings. Benzene, a component of gasoline, can damage bone marrow of inhalant abusers, keep the immune system from functioning properly, increase the risk of leukemia, and damage the reproductive system. Gasoline also contains lead, which is toxic. There are traces of lead even in unleaded gasoline. Common symptoms of low-grade lead poisoning in young people include headaches, stomachaches, nausea, lethargy, trouble sleeping, irritability, and constipation.

Harvey Weiss, executive director of the National Inhalant Prevention Coalition, finds it incredible that anyone would deliberately introduce these toxic chemicals into his or her body. "You wouldn't drink a cup of gasoline, would you?" he asks. "It's the same thing that happens when you smell these chemicals. It would poison you the same way as [drinking] gasoline."

Thirteen-year-old Sophie collapsed and died on the steps of her aunt's house after reportedly huffing gas from the tank of a four-wheeler in her tiny Alaskan village. When village health aides arrived, she was not breathing and they could not find a pulse. They started cardiopulmonary resuscitation, but their attempts to revive her failed.

METHYLENE CHLORIDE

Inhaling methylene chloride may cause skin and eye irritation. A mild central nervous system depressant, methylene chloride may cause headache, nausea, dizziness, drowsiness, loss of coordination, confusion, unconsciousness, and death. Tests on animals indicate that methylene chloride can also cause cancer.

The bodies of inhalant abusers convert methylene chloride to carbon monoxide and chloride. This combination reduces the oxygen-carrying ability of the blood and causes erratic heartbeat. Smokers and those with heart disease are particularly at risk for serious harm. Long-term exposure to fumes has been shown to cause cancer in laboratory animals. It can also cause degeneration of the myelin sheath protecting the nerve fibers of the brain.

TRICHLOROETHANE- AND TRICHLOROETHYLENE-CONTAINING PREPARATIONS

Trichloroethane vapor is a strong narcotic. Short-term exposure may irritate the nose and the eyes, cause drowsiness, loss of coordination, unconsciousness, and death. Long-term exposure may cause liver or kidney damage. Studies on animals found eye and nose irritation as well as injury to the lungs, liver, and kidneys.

Trichloroethylene causes cancer in humans. The National Institute for Occupational Safety and Health recommends that trichloroethylene in workplaces be kept to a minimum. Short-term inhalation of trichloroethylene may irritate the skin, mucous membranes, and eyes. It may also cause drowsiness, dizziness, headache, blurred vision, fatigue, loss of coordination, mental confusion, flushed skin, tremors, nausea, vomiting, and an irregular heartbeat.

Thirteen-year-old Estella probably did not think the can of cleaning fluid she was inhaling would kill her, but it did. Just a few minutes after she opened the cap and began to sniff, Estella got sick. Her parents rushed her to the hospital, where she died the next day.

Long-term inhalation may dry and blister the skin. It may also cause chronic cough, double vision, loss of the senses of touch and smell, anxiety, weakness, tremors, slowed heartbeat, and a decreased tolerance for alcohol. In animal studies acute inhalation has caused nerve, brain, liver, and kidney damage, as well as death when breathing stopped or the heart stopped beating. In humans acute inhalation has caused nerve degeneration as well as liver or kidney failure. Drinking alcohol, coffee, or other drinks containing caffeine makes the effects of exposure to chloroethylene worse. Some workers have died suddenly when their respiratory system failed, their heart began to beat erratically, or their liver or kidneys failed.

Gases

This group includes gases used in household or commercial products such as butane and propane, Freon, and nitrous oxide.

Butane and Propane

Butane is an odorless, colorless liquefied gas. Overexposure to butane fumes may cause mild irritation to the eyes and nose. It may also cause dizziness, disorientation, headache, excitation, and central nervous system depression. Extreme overexposure may cause anesthesia, unconsciousness, and respiratory arrest. As a liquefied gas, butane may cause freeze burns, but its vapors are not irritating to the skin.

Butane is a simple asphyxiant, which means that it deprives people inhaling it of oxygen. It is also explosive and flammable. Butane targets the central nervous and cardiovascular (heart and circulatory) systems. At first, inhaling butane may cause euphoria, excitation, blurred vision, slurred speech, nausea, vomiting, coughing, sneezing, and increased salivation. As people continue to inhale butane they may begin to show a loss of inhibition; confusion; perceptual distortion; hallucinations—sometimes ecstatic, sometimes terrifying—delusions, which may lead to aggressive behavior or risk taking; tinnitus (ringing in the ears); clumsiness; and lack of coordination. Large doses may lead to inability to control eye movement or speech, abnormally fast heartbeat, central nervous system depression, drowsiness, coma, and sudden death, which may result from absence of oxygen in the blood, respiratory depression, cardiac arrhythmias, or trauma. Heart failure and sudden death are especially common reactions to the abuse of butane.

Propane is a colorless, odorless gas, a byproduct of the refining of petroleum. Most propane contains a nasty-smelling chemical so that people will know when they are being exposed to the gas.

Overexposure to propane may cause dizziness and disorientation. Since propane displaces oxygen, greater exposure may cause asphyxiation, resulting in unconsciousness, and often death. Liquid propane has been known to cause frostbite. Propane is also flammable, so any spark can ignite the gas, causing fire and possible explosion.

Johnson Bryant was seventeen years old. He was a good student at a private school in Tennessee. He played varsity sports. And he made a fatal decision. In December 2001 he bought two cans of butane at a store not far from his home. He took them home, inhaled them, and died. His mother still cannot believe it. His father, with whom he was very close, still does not know why Johnson was inhaling butane. "It's frightening to see your son in a body bag," his mother told reporters. "Children just aren't supposed to die before their parents."

Inhaling high concentrations of propane, as huffers do, can lead to headache, drowsiness, fatigue, dizziness, disorientation, nausea, vomiting, mood swings, loss of coordination, suffocation, convulsions, unconsciousness, coma, and death.

The Freons

Freon is not a chemical. It is a DuPont trade name that describes a group of chemicals used in refrigeration. There are at least twenty different kinds of Freon. Most of them are composed of chlorofluorocarbons, chemicals made up of carbon and hydrogen. They also include chlorine and fluorine. The chemicals that carry the name Freon are colorless gases with a sweet odor. Each type of Freon has its own specific chemical formula. Unless someone

Fifteen-year-old Mike was almost certainly not planning to die when he and three friends decided to huff gas from a barbecue-grill propane tank in his backyard. The boys huffed the gas from a plastic bag. Mike collapsed, and died on the way to the hospital.

Rusty Quaile, thirteen, died when a propane gas tank exploded in his home. The house burned. A New Hampshire state fire marshal investigator suspected that huffing propane may have led to his death. Rusty had a history of inhalant use.

knows the exact chemical makeup of the Freon to which they have been exposed, there is no way to know what the specific health hazards will be, since some Freon are much more toxic than others.

For abusers, some Freon are more dangerous than others. Experiments on human volunteers showed that inhaling Freon 113 can change the rhythm of the heartbeat and make movement of the arms and legs difficult. Exposure to the fumes of other Freon may damage the liver, interfere with breathing, and freeze the airways, or air passages to the lungs. Often Freon abusers also burn their throats, faces, and hands. Freon—usually ethane—may also cause wildly fluctuating heartbeat and can crowd oxygen out of the lungs.

Nitrous Oxide

Nitrous oxide is also known as laughing gas, factitious air, hyponitrous acid anhydride, nitrogen oxide, and dinitrogen oxide. It is a colorless, inorganic gas with a sweet odor and taste. It is flammable, and containers may rupture in the presence of heat.

Nitrous oxide has several legitimate uses. Dentists often use so-called laughing gas to make their patients more comfortable while filling cavities and performing other dental work. Race-car drivers inject nitrous oxide into their cars' air intake systems to increase power. And the dairy industry uses nitrous oxide in cylinders to whip liquid cream into whipped cream.

Inhaling nitrous oxide may be toxic. Short-term exposure may cause nausea, vomiding, symptoms of drunkenness, hyperactivity or drowsiness, hearing loss, suffocation, and death. Long-term exposure can cause tingling sensations, impotence, and damage to the reproductive system. Contact with the skin may cause frostbite and blisters. Contact with the eyes may also cause frostbite, along with blurred vision.

Many people have experienced the effects of nitrous oxide at the dentist's office. Dentists place a mask over the nose and mouth to deliver the gas. Patients may feel a tingling in their arms and legs and hear a buzzing or humming in their ears. They feel detached from what is going on and do not feel anxiety or pain as much as they might feel without the nitrous oxide.

In the past, recreational users bought medical-grade nitrous oxide from chemical supply houses and gas companies. Today, however, supply houses will only sell to people who can prove a legitimate need. Some abusers try to fake medical or dental permits or pretend to be caterers in order to trick companies into selling it to them.

Other recreational users buy whippets—2-inch-long cylinders that dispense whipped cream—and whipped-cream charging bottles. More serious users buy nitrous oxide in tanks or make it themselves in home chemistry labs if they have the knowledge and skill.

The greatest risk associated with the casual use of nitrous oxide results from the users' lack of awareness. They may make careless mistakes that can be harmful, even deadly. First, nitrous oxide causes loss of motor control, and people who inhaled nitrous oxide have been hurt while driving or operating machinery while intoxicated. Second, nitrous oxide masks pain, so users have frozen their noses, lips, and vocal cords without even realizing they have seriously injured themselves. Third, nitrous oxide may cause confusion, nausea, or unconsciousness, so some users have inhaled their own vomit and choked to death, especially after drinking alcohol. Finally, nitrous oxide does not contain the oxygen that humans need to survive, so careless users have asphyxiated themselves by breathing nitrous oxide directly from pressurized tanks.

Serious, long-term abusers seem to develop a reverse tolerance to nitrous oxide and get more intense or prolonged feelings with a smaller amount of the drug. This leads to addiction, and addicts may experience serious mood and personality changes and may suffer bone marrow or nervous system damage. Some people who have an undiagnosed middle-ear disease or are unaware that their eardrums are damaged have experienced hearing loss—sometimes permanent—after inhaling nitrous oxide.

Nitrites

These include aliphatic nitrites, found in room odorizers; amyl nitrite, which is available only by prescription; and butyl nitrite, now an illegal substance.

Unlike other inhalants, which are abused mainly for their intoxicating effects, nitrites are abused primarily because they are believed to enhance sexual pleasure and performance. Nitrites are among the inhalants that frequently cause sudden death. Inhaled nitrites may dilate blood vessels, increase heart rate, and produce a sensation of heat and

Renee Sherer wants students everywhere to know that inhaling the nitrites in aerosol fumes can kill. She knows because her twelve-year-old son, Tyler, died when he experimented with inhaling fumes from an aerosol can. Sniffing nitrites was not uncommon among Tyler's friends. Several girls told Mrs. Sherer at Tyler's memorial service that they regularly carried cans of whipped cream in their purses and huffed in the bathroom at school.

excitement that can last for several minutes. Other effects may include flushing, dizziness, and headache.

With all the information available about how poisonous these chemicals are, it is amazing that anyone would choose to inhale them deliberately.

Most inhalant users never make it to the emergency room, but if they do, they are very, very ill and need specialized treatment.

4 Help for Inhalant Abusers

MANY TEENS ARE aware of classmates and close friends who are abusing inhalants. But others have no idea what the warning signs are. Robert lost his thirteen-year-old brother to inhalants and only learned the indicators of inhalant abuse after his brother was dead. "I wish that I could have told my brother [about inhalants]," Bob wrote. "Maybe if I had, he would have made a no-use decision . . . and he would be alive today."

Teens who suspect that a family member, friend, or classmate is abusing inhalants can do something to help. Talking to a parent, teacher, or school counselor may not seem cool, but it could prevent a

Signs of Inhalant Abuse

- Problems in school—falling grades, skipping class
- A sudden "I-don't-care" attitude
- Loss of interest in friends and family, clothing, grooming, and hobbies
- Paint stains on body or clothing
- Spots or sores around the mouth
- Red or runny eyes or nose
- Chemical breath odor
- Loss of appetite
- Nausea
- Anxiety or excitability
- Unusual irritability
- A drunk, dazed, or dizzy appearance
- Bad headaches
- An ongoing cough
- Shaky hands

tragedy. Knowing the facts about inhalants and talking openly about them is also important. So is being brave enough to tell a friend, "Don't start. It's not worth it."

Teens who find a friend suffering from acute inhalant intoxication or inhalant overdose should stay calm and not panic, as this will cause increased stress. People who are under the influence of inhalants can become aggressive or violent, so it is important not to argue with, or excite, them. Stress or excitement may lead to more violence, hallucinations, or even Sudden Sniffing Death, in which the inhalant user's heart stops suddenly.

Whether the person is conscious or unconscious, teens should calmly summon help—sending for an adult or calling 911. While waiting for help, teens should stay calm and open windows and doors so fresh air can disperse any chemical fumes. In order for professionals to treat an inhalant overdose, it is helpful to know exactly what substance the user overdosed on. Saving evidence or finding out what a friend was inhaling may be very helpful. And finally, friends should talk to friends about getting long-term help for their inhalant abuse, encouraging them to talk with a school nurse, counselor, family physician, or other health-care worker.

Emergency Treatment

Most inhalant abusers never end up in an emergency room. When they do, they are generally very sick and need specialized treatment.

When patients arrive at an emergency room after overdosing on inhalants, the medical staff immediately makes sure that they can breathe and that they do not inhale any fluids into their lungs. They start a flow of oxygen via a mask or a tube inserted into the lungs. They monitor vital signs and heartbeat and insert an IV in case they need to administer emergency drugs for irregular heartbeat or other complications. If patients have swallowed other drugs, the medical staff will most likely pump the stomach.

Knowing what patients have been inhaling, and for how long, may mean the difference between life and death. If family members or friends are present, the staff will probably ask how much, and for how long, patients have been inhaling. Have there been recent changes in behavior or problems at school? Have patients acted out of control or tried dangerous activities? Is it possible they have swallowed other types of drugs?

Doctors may order chest X-rays to look for pneumonia, enlarged heart, or pulmonary edema—an accumulation of fluids in the lungs. Sophisticated scans of the head can show bleeding in the brain, hidden fractures, and brain atrophy. An electrocardiograph (EKG) monitors the heart for irregular rhythms. Doctors may also order lab tests to see how much oxygen there is in the blood and how the lungs are functioning, to check for levels of certain chemicals in the body, to check for liver or kidney damage, and to look for damage to the blood.

Throughout treatment the emergency-room staff will try to keep patients calm, since fear and inhalants both raise blood pressure and increase the heart rate. Apart from these steps, there is little that emergency medical personnel can do for patients suffering from inhalant overdose. If patients survive, withdrawal from acute inhalant intoxication takes from two to five days or longer. Patients may experience sleep disturbance, tremors, nausea, irritability, and abdominal pain. They may become delirious, with confused speech and hallucinations. There is no medication that can speed up withdrawal.

Long-Term Treatment

People who abuse inhalants are often a hidden group. They are unlike other people who are chemically dependent. They are easy to overlook and do not receive treatment as often, so inhalant abuse often goes undetected. They also have unique treatment needs. Inhalant abusers need programs with staff members knowledgeable about their particular problem, people who understand how long recovery can take and that relapse is common.

Although more than two million young people have admitted to using inhalants in their lifetime, only a tiny fraction of inhalant abusers ever make it into treatment. Of 131,000 teens admitted to treatment centers in 1999, only 569 reported that inhalants were the main substance they abused. Another 1,422 reported abuse of inhalants along with the abuse of other drugs.

Treatment programs have to treat the physical symptoms of inhalant abusers before they can treat the psychological effects of addiction. Treatment counselors have to do complicated medical tests to find out what chemicals patients have been using and how much damage they have done to their bodies and brains. They have to provide time for detoxification from the immediate effects of inhalants—from two to six weeks or more.

Since most inhalants target the brain, patients often have serious cognitive (thinking) problems. After detoxification, treatment programs have to test cognitive function to see how much deterioration has taken place. Throughout, programs have to keep intervention sessions short and simple, since most patients no longer have a normal attention span. Some are erratic, disruptive, and occasionally violent.

Treatment counselors have to treat the serious psychological problems of inhalant abusers. Why were they attracted to inhalants in the first place? What are their families like?

Will the families have a positive or negative influence on treatment? What basic life skills do patients have? Can they bond with other people? Is there a negative peer group that will undo treatment once patients go home? What kind of physical, emotional, or sexual abuse have they suffered?

Inhalant treatment has to incorporate prevention education into the program, since many people in treatment do not realize how toxic inhalants are. Patients' families need education as well. Removing inhalants from the home and providing extra support and supervision is critical. So is a school-based advocate or counselor, who can give the recovering abuser special attention and support.

A High Rate of Failure

All these things are difficult, expensive, and time-consuming, which is part of the reason why standard drug treatment is not generally successful with inhalant abusers. Most drug treatment centers use alcohol and drug treatment techniques with inhalant abusers, techniques that do not take into account that inhalant abusers are different from abusers of other substances.

Treatment centers that have been successful with other addictions may not realize that their premises are a storehouse packed with drugs for inhalant abusers. Programs that would never consider leaving a stash of marijuana or Ecstasy out for their patients barely consider locking up dry-erase markers, nail polish, and solvent-based glues. It does not occur to them that plastic bags and party balloons are drug paraphernalia.

Ricky Stem's Story

On March 15, 2001, Diane Stem kicked off the National Inhalants & Poisons Awareness Week with the story of her sixteen-year-old son's death. "Ricky was an outgoing sixteen-year-old," she said. "He loved listening to music, talking with his friends on the phone, and sports. He had a passion for baseball since the age of four, when the bat was still bigger than he was." The left-handed, all-state pitcher on his school's baseball team had already earned the attention of university and professional scouts. His father, Ricky Sr., and he liked to dream of a bright future in the world of sports.

The dream died just after Ricky's sophomore year in high school. On June 20, 1996, Ricky Sr. came home from work to find his only son dead in his room. Ricky had been huffing Freon from the home air-conditioning unit. "Our son didn't know he had invited a killer into our home that day," Mrs. Stem said. "He never meant to hurt anyone, let alone himself. Harmless fun."

But there is hope. In 2002 the nation's first treatment center dedicated to inhalant abuse opened in Bethel, Alaska. "We are hopeful that what we learn in Alaska can be translated into treatment protocols that can be used in all fifty states to treat inhalant abuse," said Dr. H. Westley Clark, director of the Center for Substance Abuse Treatment.

Government Agencies

Each year, the National Inhalant Prevention Coalition observes National Inhalants & Poisons Awareness Week in March. More than eight hundred public, private, and governmental organizations from forty-six states participated in the last campaign.

As is often the case with substance abuse, the best deterrent is education. National Families in Action—a national drug education, prevention, and policy center—helps families and communities prevent drug abuse among children.

5 Inhalants and the Law

PERHAPS THE VERY first law concerning inhalants was Ordinance Number 1722, passed by the city of Anaheim, California, on June 6, 1962. This ordinance made it illegal for any person to:

> inhale, breathe, or drink any compound, liquid, chemical, or any substance known as glue, adhesive cement, mucilage, dope, or other material or substance or combination thereof, with the intention of becoming intoxicated, elated, dazed, paralyzed, irrational or in any manner changing, distorting or disturbing the eyesight, thinking process, balance, or coordination of such person.

A 1962 Maryland law made it:

> unlawful for any person under twenty-one years of age to deliberately smell or inhale such excessive quantities of any narcotics, drugs, or any other noxious substances or chemicals containing any ketones, aldehydes, organic acetates, ether, chlorinated hydrocarbons or any other substances containing solvents releasing toxic vapors, as cause conditions of intoxication, inebriation, excitement, stupefaction, or dulling of the brain and nervous system. . . . Any person violating this section will be guilty of a misdemeanor and upon conviction thereof shall be fined.

By 1968 thirteen states and twenty-nine counties and municipalities had already passed glue-sniffing laws and had many more under consideration.

The first effort to repress the recreational use of nitrous oxide (laughing gas) was instituted in 1971. *Psychiatric News* reported:

> Strict regulations have been placed on the distribution and sale of nitrous oxide in Maryland by Dr. Neil Solomon, state secretary of health and mental hygiene, following reports that the gas is being used by some young people as an inhalant to produce an exhilarating effect. This is the first regulatory action taken in the nation concerning improper use of nitrous oxide, according to information from the Food and Drug Administration. . .

Although the federal Controlled Substances Act, passed in 1970, does not address inhalant abuse, many state legislatures have attempted to deter youth who buy legal products to get high by placing restrictions on the sale of these products to minors. The main problem in passing laws is that the laws cannot ban inhalants in the same way as they ban other drugs such as marijuana or heroin.

According to a report by the National Conference of State Legislatures, some states have introduced fines, prison sentences, or mandatory treatment for the sale, distribution, use, and/or possession of inhalable chemicals. Thirty-eight states have adopted laws preventing the sale, use, and/or distribution to minors of various products commonly abused as inhalants. Twelve states ban sales of inhalants to minors outright. Two ban sales or distribution for the purpose of intoxication. Twenty-five states have made inhaling certain compounds for the purpose of intoxication illegal. Texas makes it illegal to possess, sell, or buy volatile chemicals that can be abused. Nebraska and Massachusetts businesses must maintain a register of sales of inhalants. Texas and Minnesota require businesses to post signs warning of the dangers of abusing inhalants. Massachusetts requires buyers to provide identification and requires that makers of inhalants include "noxious deterrents"—chemical additives that will make inhaling unpleasant or painful.

Even when states, cities, or counties have anti-inhalant laws on the books, prosecution of offenders tends to be minimal. However, several states use existing laws that make it illegal to drive under the influence of alcohol and drugs to prosecute those who drive under the influence of inhalants, and New Jersey recently added inhalants to its law.

Inhalants and the War on Drugs

Inhalants have been overlooked in the War on Drugs. However, inhalants do seem to contribute to the kind of behavior that lands people in jail. The 1997 Bureau of Justice Statistics Survey of Inmates in State and Federal Correctional Facilities reports that 7.7 percent of federal prisoners had tried inhalants in their lifetime; 2.6 percent had used inhalants regularly; and 0.5% had used inhalants in the month before committing the offense for which they went to jail. Almost 15 percent of state prisoners nationwide had tried inhalants in their lifetime, 5.4 percent had used inhalants regularly, and 1 percent had used inhalants in the month before committing their offense.

Today, many states consider the War on Drugs too expensive, both in terms of the cost of incarceration and of lives wasted in prison. For example, many state courts have begun to impose fines or order treatment rather than impose long prison sentences for simple possession of marijuana. This is important, since it is state and local police who make most drug arrests in the U.S. and local courts who deal with drug abusers. It also makes more sense to treat people rather than to put them in jail.

These changes may have some effect on the way states deal with inhalant abusers.

However, inhalant abuse has always been a faint blip on the drug war's radar. It will probably continue to be. Products containing inhalants will continue to be legal and commonplace. Abusers will continue to be prosecuted only when they bring themselves to the attention of authorities through dangerous or antisocial behavior.

But the hope is that nationwide anti-inhalant campaigns will continue to bring the problem of inhalant abuse to light; that parents, teachers, and doctors will begin to recognize warning signs; and that young people—realizing that inhalants can destroy their lives—will decide that inhaling poisonous chemicals is just not worth it.

Glossary

anesthetic: An agent that causes loss of feeling or sensation.

bagging: Pouring a substance into a plastic bag and inhaling the fumes.

central nervous system: The brain and spinal cord.

dopamine: Neurotransmitter present in regions of the brain that regulate movement, emotion, motivation, and feeling of pleasure.

huffing: Putting a rag soaked in a substance over the nose and mouth and inhaling.

psychoactive: Mind-altering.

Sudden Sniffing Death: reaction to inhaling toxins in which the heart beats irregularly and then stops.

toxic: Poisonous.

volatile solvents: Liquids that produce chemical gases at room temperature.

withdrawal: Symptoms that occur after use of an addictive drug is reduced or stopped.

Further Information

Where to Get Help
National Inhalant Prevention Coalition
1-800-269-4237

Web Sites
National Inhalant Prevention Coalition
www.inhalants.org/

Inhalant Abuse Prevention
www.inhalant.org

Parents: The Anti-DrugDrug Information: Inhalants
www.theantidrug.com/drug_info/drugs_inhalants.html

Office of National Drug Control Policy: Drug Policy Information Clearinghouse
www.whitehousedrugpolicy.gov/publications/factsht/inhalants/index.html>

Books

Chier, Ruth. *Danger: Inhalants.* New York: PowerKids Press, 1996.

Fitzhugh, Karla. *Inhalants.* Austin, TX: Raintree-Steck Vaughn Publishers, 2003.

Monroe, Judy. *Inhalant Drug Dangers.* Springfield, NJ: Enslow Publishers, Inc., 1999.

O'Donnell, Kerri. *Inhalants and Your Nasal Passages: The Incredibly Disgusting Story.* New York: Rosen Central, 2001.

Royston, Angela. *Inhalants.* Chicago: Heinemann Library, 2000.

Sherry, Clifford J. *Inhalants.* New York: Rosen Publishing Group, 1997.

Bibliography

Brecher, Edward M. *Licit and Illicit Drugs: The Consumers Union Report on Narcotics, Stimulants, Depressants, Inhalants, Hallucinogens, and Marijuana*. Boston: Little, Brown & Co., 1972.

"Huffing: The Abuse of Inhalants." Intelligence Brief: November 2001. National Drug Intelligence Center, U.S. Department of Justice, Johnstown, PA.

Landry, Mim J. *Understanding Drugs of Abuse: The Processes of Addiction, Treatment, and Recovery*. Washington, DC: American Psychiatric Press, 1994.

Weil, Andrew. *From Chocolate to Morphine: Everything You Need to Know about Mind-Altering Drugs*. Boston: Houghton Mifflin, 1993.

INDEX

Page numbers in boldface are illustrations and tables.

abuse signs, 14, 16–17, 19, 63–64, 67
addiction, 12, 16, 20–21, 49, 59, 68
adhesives, 8, 10, 13, 30–33, 38
aerosols, 10, 30, 33, 36, 60
age, 15, 18, 34–37, **35**, 74
air freshener, 10
Alaska, 71
alcohol, 53
aliphatic nitrites, 60
amyl nitrite, 13, 60
anesthetics, 10, 28
See also nitrous oxide
antifreeze, 10
anxiety, 53, 58, 64

appetite, 64
asphyxiants, 54–55, 58–59
attention span, 68

benzene, 47, 51
blood, 46, **47**, 52
blood pressure, 67
blood vessels, 60–61
bone marrow, 44, 47, 59
brain, 10, 18, 21, 31, 32, 44, **45**, 48, 52
  cerebellum, **46**
  cerebral cortex, **46**
breathing, 19, 46, 55, 57
butane, 54
butyl nitrite, 60

caffeine, 53
Canadian Centre for Occupational Health and Safety, 45
cancer, 47, 50, 51, 52
carbon monoxide, 52
caulking compounds, 10
cement, 32
Central America, 38–39, **40**
central nervous system, 54
chemicals, 10, 12, 44–45, 56–57, 74
chlorofluorocarbons, 56–57
chloroform, 10, 28
choking, 59
chronic use, 44
cleaning fluids, **6**, 9
clothing, 64
clues, of use, 14, 16–17, 19, 63–64, 67
coma, 55, 56
confusion, 52, 53, 56, 59, 64, 67
Controlled Substances Act, 74
convulsions, 56
coordination, 44, 46, 49, 52, 54, 56, 57
correction fluid, 6, 30
coughing, 19, 53, 54

crimes, 75
danger, 8, **11**, 20, 24,
 31–32, 59
Davy, Humphry, 28, **29**
deaths, 10, 16, 22–25,
 33, 39, **43**, 51, 53, 55,
 56, 60, 70
 Sudden Sniffing
 Death, 25, 47, 60,
 65
delirium, 67
delusions, 54
dementia, 44
depressants, 52
depression, 48, 49
detachment, 58, 64
detection, 14, 16–17, 19,
 63–64, 67
deterrents, 74
detoxification period,
 68
difluoroethane, 22–23
dinitrogen oxide.
 See nitrous oxide
dizziness, 50, 51, 53, 61
dopamine, 21
driving, 22–23, 59, 75
Drug Abuse Warning
 Network (DAWN), 24

ears, 59
 See also hearing
education, 69, 71, 76
 books, 82–84
 Web sites, 81–82
epidemics, 31–33
ether, 10, 28
ether frolics, 28
euphoria, 19, 20–21
 See also highs
excitability, 64, 65
explosives, 54–56
eyes, 52, 53, 64
 vision, 19, 44, 49, 53,
 54, 58

factitious air.
 See nitrous oxide
families, 16–17, 63–65,
 68–69
feeling, loss of, 49, 53
fire, 49, 50, 54, 55

flushing, 53, 61
Freons, 56–57, 70
friends, 18–20, 36, 63–65

gases, 54–59
gasoline, 10, 30, 49–51
gender factor, 15
glue-sniffing, 30–33, 38, 47
grades, 15, 64

hallucinations, 19, 46, 54, 67
halothane, 10
hearing, 44, 47, 58
  buzzing sound, 58
  ringing sounds, 54
heart, 10, 25, 33, 44, 46, **47**, 48, 53, 55, 57, 67
help
  for friends, 63, 65
  phone number, 81
highs, 19, 20–21, 24, 28, 33, 43, 50, 54, 60–61
history
  ancient times, **26**, 27–28
laws, 72–75 (*see also* laws)
nineteenth century, 28, 30
after World War II, 30–33
Hobby Industry Association, 31
home laboratories, 59
household products, **6**, 7–8
hunger, 38–39
hyperactivity, 58
hyponitrous acid anhydride. *See* nitrous oxide

Industrial Revolution, 30
industrial toxins, 45
inhibitions, loss of, 24, 28, 44, 54
inks, 10
insomnia, 51
interactions, 53

intoxication, 58, 64, 65, 72
inventions, 30
irritability.
See personality change
isobutyl nitrite, 13
judgment, 24, 28, 50, 54

kidneys, 44, 48, 52, 53

labels, 12, 36, **42**
laughing gas.
See nitrous oxide
laws, 9, 11, 12, 20, 31, 60, 72–75
lead poisoning, 51
learning ability, 15, 46, 64
leukemia, 47, 51
lighter fluid, 10
liver, 10, 32, 44, **45**, 46, **47**, 48, 52, 53, 57
long-term use, 44, 52, 59
lungs, 19, 44, 46, **47**, 52, 57

media, 30–33
medical substances, 10, 28
memory, 46
methylene chloride, 52
minors, 74
See also age
mood swings, 56, 59
mouth, 53, 64
muscles, 47
myelin, 49, 52

nail polish, 10
narcotics, 52–53
National Inhalant Prevention Coalition, 71
phone number, 81
National Institute for Occupational Safety and Health (NIOSH), 45
Native Americans, 14
nerves, 49, 52, 53
nervous system, 19, 21, 44, 48, 50, 59
nitrites, 10, 13, 60–61

nitrous oxide, 10, 13, 28, 57–59, 73
nose, 52, 59, 64

Occupational Safety and Health Administration (OSHA), 45
office supplies, 9, 22
Oracle of Delphi, **26**, 27–28
oxygen, 46, 52, 55, 59

pain, 59, 67
paint thinners, **6**, 9, 10
peer pressure, 18–20, 36
personality change, 44, 46, 51, 54, 59, 64, 65, 66, 67, 68
Plutarch, 27–28
poets, 28–30
possession, 74
poverty, 38–39, **40**
pregnancy, 39, 44, 48
prevention, 69
  See also education
propane, 55–56
prosecution, 75
publicity, 30–33, 71, 76

recreational drugs, 10, 12, 21
refrigerants, 56–57, 70
reproductive organs, 58
risk taking. *See* judgment
room deodorizers, 60
Rossetti, Dante Gabriel, 28–30
rubber, 10
safety, **11**, 12, 36, **42**, 43, 45–48
salivation, 54
schools, 69
sealants, 10
sex, 58, 60
skin
  blisters, 58
  burns, 57
  discoloration, 19

flushing, 53, 61
frostbite, 55, 58, 59
rashes, 47, 52–53
slang, 13
sleep, 67
smell
breath odor, 64
sense of, 53
smokers, 50, 52
socioeconomic factors, 15, 38–39, **40**
solvents, 48–53
speech, 19, 44, 46, 54
spray paint, 10
sprays, 10, 30, 33
state laws, 73–76
street names, 7, 13
Substance Abuse and Mental Health Services Administration (SAMHSA), 34
Sudden Sniffing Death syndrome, 25, 47, 55
suicide, 24, 49
suppliers, 38, 58, 74
symptoms
of use, 19, 43–45, 50, 52, 53, 54–56, 58, 60–61
of withdrawal, 20, 67

taste, sense of, 39
terminology, 13
thinking, 44, 49, 68
tinnitus, 54
tolerance, 20, 59
toluene, 10, 21, 38, 48–49
treatment
in emergencies, 12, **62**, 65–67
failures, 49, 69
long-term, 67–69
treatment centers, 69–71
tremors, 19, 46, 53, 64, 67
trends, 34–41, **35**
trichloroethane, 52
trichloroethylene, 10, 52–53

urinary excretion, 21
users
  characteristics, 14–15
  motivation, 18–20, 36
  names for, 13
  number of, 34–41, **35**, 67
  social *vs.* isolate, 18
  talking to, 65
  in treatment, 67–68

vomiting, 53, 54, 56, 58, 59

walking, 49
warnings, 12, 36, **42**, 43, 45–48
War on Drugs, 75–76
Web sites, 81–82
whipped cream, 57, 58
withdrawal, 20, 67
workplace, **11**, 45, 48, 52–53

ABOUT THE AUTHOR

Francha Roffé Menhard was a teacher for more than twenty-five years in both the United States and Japan. She has written advertisements, books, and newspaper columns. Ms. Menhard enjoys traveling, genealogy, and scrapbooking. She lives with her family and one foreign exchange student in the shadow of the Rocky Mountains.